black fen

poetry

alex brockhurst

tall-lighthouse

for Boris & in memory of my father

The author would like to thank Julia Ball, Brendan Cleary, Andrew Flower, Deborah Leech, Rory Singer, Marie Thompson & Richard Thorn for their kindness & support.

Acknowledgements: some of these poems have appeared in *automatic lighthouse* and *The Slab*

Cover image: ghost light - alex brockhurst

Cover photo: rachael adams

Cover design from an original concept by Suman

© Alex Brockhurst 2009
Alex Brockhurst has asserted her rights under the Copyright, Design & Patents Act 1988 to be identified as the author of this work.

published 2009
ISBN 978 1 904551 62 1
www.tall-lighthouse.co.uk

contents

Fallen	1
Rain	2
Silence	3
Window	4
Signs	5
Black Fen	6
April	7
Wolstonbury	8
These days	11
Here again	12
Platform 3	13
Prayer	14
Over	15
Only now	16
Hard stuff	17
Costa Brava	18
By the pool	19
Daydream	20
After you go	21
Space	22
Still waiting	23

All that is mine
beloved and pleasing
will become otherwise
will become separated from me

(Dasadhamma Sutta, Ang.10)

Fallen

See my coat
lying on the stairs

the pockets
empty of stars

see your light
behind curtains

drawn to reveal
a panel of day

divided by shadow
& look — no hands

my fall
is effortless

Rain

Quiet beyond
belief

beyond
expression

you stand
out there

a spit
of rocky shore

shouting
at the waves

the simple sea
trying hard

to follow
what you say

hears only
gentle rain

relentless
as we brace ourselves

Silence

Just now
the scouring

wind & salt
will crumble fast

these sediments
betrayed beneath

your troubled face
a sharpening pain

that tears my gut
so sore

with tiring sympathy
I bite my tongue

Window

There never was
much else to do

much other than
see through this

backroom window
bright *cotinus*

gleaming coins
my solitude

before this deep
relentless ivy

& black bamboo
you measured with me

noting day by day
its urgent reach

for space
regardless

Signs

I will collect
these dead

geranium
leaves

make signs
of them

finding
their lightness

as they crackle
in my hands

& see
the new leaves

coming without
my willing

green & more
so green

Black Fen

& where is this
we stop

silhouetted
along the track

our eyes transfixed
at the skyline

as the wind picks up
a mistimed note

my heart gives out
this shaking beat

& I grow giddy
in a blast of cold

that shifts the light
to whisper why

we've stopped
on this bleak track

April

& sometimes you go by
too quickly

not seeing the violets
so very near the ground

hitting the middle distance
foot following foot

judging the day fine
& rather dry for April

& you miss the particular
way of things

their readiness before
we are quite upon them

the tenderest shoots
setting to go no matter what

& missed if we wait
a moment longer

Wolstonbury

i

Then there is
only this

the wide green
pitched

against the grey
macadam

& the mist
drawing

down over
Wolstonbury

& the dog
wistful of the water

standing alert
at the barbed wire

her eyes so far
across the fields

ii

With empty hands
I come to this

surefooted
in the greylight

sinking in
to sodden turf

as heaving clouds
roll down on us

a sudden turn
she gazes back

along our tracks
& sits expectant

the trees
already knowing

their shape
against the wind

iii

What is it
I say to her

she seems
content to wait

for something
to be settled

a following
footfall

absent
in the moment

as I urge her on
towards the wood

pale lichen
clads the bark

of darkening
trees

These days

A second later
& it's gone

old nutshells rattling
these deep pockets

nostalgia for
some other days

walking the towpath
unfamiliar

the riverboats
mooring other lives

to these
rainclouded ways

Here again

Nothing standing
as it did before

I recognise the trees
the curve & straight

of once familiar
landscape

baffling my eyes
in this coming mist

& see less certainty
about the place

I once held out
as home

Platform 3

This landscape
of leaving

a place so lonely
the flowers

silt grey
bloom silent

in shadows
& cluster

for comfort
in dust

without rain
quickly fading

Prayer

Make of me
some use

just here
between the bed

the curtain
& the sky

& thread me up
a string of beads

joining this
to that again

not fearing
for your tread

upon the stair
that brings

the gift
of your concern

into the room
as I lie waking

Over

What can I
tell you

the sky will
always be blue

last month's lilies
wilt in the vase

& pollen stains
my hand

as I brush past
vivid on my skin

& will not wash away
til afternoon

Only now

Just this way
of things

the shape
& purpose

place & span
no way other

than this pain
that hurt

this very moment
then the next

Hard stuff

Watching you
lately

& thinking about
that thing

you do
with your hand

like it hesitates
to touch

such fragile
things

not wanting
to break them

like you break
everything else

without touching
a drop

Costa Brava

Eleven forty-five
shutters closed

door ajar
echoes of crockery

& laughter
down the valley

automatic sprinklers
whisper & repeat

a sound so close
yet still remote

murmuring
regret

your measured voice
on the terrace below

the gentle mutter
of making up

By the pool

I only came
to watch she said

a finger
tracing along

the fine line
separating

blue dark
eyes narrowing

the view
removing her

further out
of bounds

the angular
shift from

restraint
to certainty

I won't go in
just now she said

Daydream

& I'm lying on your couch
in semi-darkness

watching for your feet
& with my face

here like this — down
is the only place I'm looking

& around comes your body
& my own

becomes this landscape
in your hands

drawing deep into the current
sweeping nearer to the rocks

& so willing is my breath
it must betray me

as I wonder how
to put on these clothes

After you go

Clothes strewn
across the chair

shadows mingle
as music fails

& you're not here
to play the other side

& I'm not quite
warm enough

without you
as I move

to straighten & fold
replace the dress

brought out
for you

must be
two nights ago

Space

Some while after
the door clicks shut

imagining a place
without you

wondering
just how it could be

feeling the space
how white & soft

so light a touch
without your boots

Still waiting
(i.m. D.I.T.)

Ushered through
curtains

to the wing
I wait to face

my final audience
with you

& so sudden
comes the moment

of our meeting
lines are senseless

my hand so warm
on your cold shoulder

I'm believing
though your blood

has ruptured
into bloom

that you will still
be waiting

in some other
shaded room